THE RECIPES OF THE MAFIA
The secret plates of the 'Ndrangheta

By Lino Ponte

Illustration: Maria Lupina
Editing: Meliviona Gratsia

Copyright © 2014 by Lino Ponte

Table of contents

Puglia

Calabria

+
Polsi

Sicily

What is the 'Ndrangheta

The 'Ndrangheta is an ancient criminal organization active both inside and outside Italian territory. It first appeared in Calabria but nowadays it has roots in various other regions of Italy with worldwide connections (South America, United States, Australia, Eastern and Western Europe etc.) and ramifications.

The most probable derivation of the term 'Ndrangheta is from the Greek word "andragathia", which can be translated as "manliness", "braveness" (a term cited in this meaning by Thomas Aquinas in his "Summa Theologica) in the sense of the "organization of brave men". Indeed "andragathos" is a man with valor and courage. Only this man with these values would be able to have access to this "onorata societa". The 'Ndrangheta earns more than Deutche Bank and McDonalds put together. In Italy alone it brings in about 27 billion euros per year through drug and arm smuggling.

The Sanctuary "Madonna di Polsi"

The Sanctuary of the 'Ndrangheta

In these few pages you can find the recipes that are part of the codes of "life and death" ("vita e morte") that were recovered by the Italian Police in an anti-mafia operation organized in Calabria in 2010, on the grounds of the Sanctuary of Madonna di Polsi or Madonna of the Mountains. The "codes" are manuscripts that are used by members of the society to hand down the rituals used for the administration of the criminal organization.

The rituals of the 'Ndrangheta are the necessary procedures in order to enter the criminal organization (baptism etc). Being a secret society, throughout its history, it has developed different rituals for every occasion. Additionally, it is the only criminal organization of the mafia that has maintained the rituals that distinguish it from the past.

A lot of stories are told about the "Madonna di Polsi". One of these recounts that in the 9th century several byzantine monks, running away from nearby Sicily due to invasions by the Saracens, found refuge at the heart of Aspromonte, at the root of the mountain, where they founded a small colony and a church.

Another very popular story says that during the 11th century a shepherd named Italiano, from the small town of Santa Cristina d' Aspromonte, while looking for a lost bull, saw the animal unearth an iron cross. At that moment Madonna with baby Jesus appeared saying that she wants a church to be built for her grace to become known to all those who come and visit her.

Nowadays in the interior of the sanctuary the statue of the "Madonna della Montagna" of Polsi is preserved, as well as sculptures of extreme beauty and brilliance, the Cross and various other memorabilia amongst which is the casket of the prince of the area.

Therefore, the sanctuary of "Madonna di Polsi" is of immense importance to the 'Ndrangheta, the Calabrian mafia. Every year, during the feast of the Madonna, the bosses of the 'Ndrangheta, not only from Calabria but from the whole world, get together to eat. On this occasion extremely important decisions are made. Alliances are formed, wars are declared and criminal strategies are planned. It is believed that the decision to kill Francesco Fortugno (an Italian politician), the German massacre of 15th August 2007 and many others were made in Polsi. These are the two faces of Polsi, the combination of good and bad, which, in this case, live one alongside the other in perfect harmony.

Nicola Gratteri, a judge dedicated to the 'Ndrangheta war, has said about Polsi: "Every year, in September, the heads of mafia reunite in Polsi to discuss the criminal strategies. They assign the appointment of new members, the judgements, they decide to open or close a "branch" of the 'Ndrangheta. "They reuinite in Polsi because it's a sacred place, the place of the preservation of the 12 tables of the 'Ndrangheta… because the power of the "Santa" (another name to describe the 'Ndrangheta) compared to other criminal organizations is that it respects the rules in a strict way".

Madonna della Montagna

The Tree of Knowledge

The Tree of Knowledge

We should also mention the so-called "Albero della Scienza" (Tree of Knowledge). Used for various rituals, this huge tree is situated in the garden of the sanctuary and is strongly linked to its history. The Tree of Knowledge is a metaphor of how the mafia society is structured: from a code discovered during an affiliation ritual it was revealed that the Tree of Knowledge is divided in 6 parts:

The trunk represents the boss of the society; the branches are the members of the mafia; the smaller branches stand for the "picciotti" (young men found at the very basic level of a mafia organization) and the blossoms represent the "young men of honour" (accountants); the leaves represent the traitors of the 'Ndrangheta that rot under the Tree of Knowledge.

At the base of the tree there is also a grave that symbolizes the end of the leaves.
In the code of the 'Ndrangheta the tree is shown as a "little garden of roses and flowers" with a star in the middle where "picciotti" and young men of honour are baptized. The "picciotto" enters the little garden with open eyes, with chains on the arms and legs in the grave.

The recipes

In the history of the Mafia, meals are as important as in Gospels: The mafia meal is a liturgy. These are the recipes of the meals during which the future of some people was decided or which are connected with historical moments.

These are the selected plates from the actual bosses of the families of the 'Ndrangheta. This means that the "Ricettario" is a list of recipes that varies according to the personality of each "capo" that directs the organization of the Santa.

The value of these pages doesn't derive from the recipes, which even though not very elaborate are indeed very tasty, but rather from the fact that these are the evidence of a secret "tradition" that is still unknown and difficult to understand even today.

IL RICETTARIO

Macaroni

Ingredients for 4 servings:
500g semolina flour
water
olive oil
salt

In Calabria macaroni are traditionally made at home. The pasta is rolled using a "Ferretti", a long and very fine round wooden stick.

Mix the semolina flour with tepid water, a pinch of salt and a few drops of olive oil and knead until you get a soft and elastic dough. Let it rest for an hour in a dry place, then cut it into small pieces. Roll out each piece with the "Ferretti" to make fine macaroni. When done, let them dry. Boil the pasta into salted water and drain when it's "al dente". Dress it with tomato or minced pork sauce, adding a lot of grated cheese.

Macaroni with ricotta cheese

Ingredients for 4 servings:
500 g macaroni
250g fresh ricotta cheese
1 tablespoon lard
salted grated ricotta (to taste)
black pepper

Prepare the macaroni as described in the previous recipe. Boil the pasta "al dente". Keep a glass of the pasta water apart and then strain it. Mix the macaroni with the fresh ricotta, the melted lard, the pasta water, some black pepper and salted grated ricotta to taste. Mix well and serve hot.

Spaghetti with cuttlefish sauce

Ingredients for 4 servings:
500g spaghetti
800g fresh cuttlefish
3 tomatoes
olive oil
salt
pepper
parsley
1 chili pepper

To cook this dish it's important that the cuttle-fish be fresh. Rinse the fish well and heat it in a pan with some oil. Peel the tomatoes, remove the seeds, chop and add them to the pan. Add the chili pepper, a tablespoon of chopped parsley, salt and pepper. Cover the pan and cook in low heat for 20 minutes. Remove the fish and keep it warm to serve as second course. Boil the spaghetti "al dente" and mix it with the sauce.

Spaghetti with pilchards

Ingredients for 4 servings:
500g spaghetti
6 fillets of salted pilchards
1k peeled tomatoes
2 garlic cloves
1 onion
4 tablespoons breadcrumbs
2 tablespoons parsley chopped
olive oil

salt

Sauté the garlic cloves and the onion sliced fine into a pan with olive oil. Add the salted pilchards fillets and let them cook until they melt. Add the chopped tomatoes, salt and pepper to taste and cook the sauce in low heat for at least one hour. Slightly toast the breadcrumbs into a pan greased with olive oil. Boil the pasta "al dente", drain it and add the sauce and the toasted breadcrumbs. Serve hot.

Pork rolls

Ingredients for 5 servings:
1k pork meat without fat
250g pork lard in small pieces
300g pecorino cheese in cubes
garlic
olive oil
salt
pepper
parsley

kitchen string

Cut the pork meat into medium-thick slices. On each slice place some lard pieces, pecorino cheese cubes, garlic slices, chopped parsley, salt and pepper. Turn the pork slices into small rolls and tie each one with kitchen string. Fry in a pan with hot olive oil. Serve as it is or simmer the fried rolls into tomato sauce, which can then be used as sauce for pasta.

Pan-cooked pilchards

Ingredients for 4 servings:
1k fresh pilchards
oregano
salt
pepper
olive oil

1 glass white vinegar

Fillet the pilchards and place them into a pan.
Sprinkle them with lots of oregano and pepper,
add a pinch of salt and dampen with some olive
oil and vinegar. Partly cover the pan and cook in
medium heat for 15 minutes.

Fried pilchards

Ingredients for 4 servings:
1k fresh pilchards (medium size)
½ glass white vinegar
white vinegar (for marinade)
water
1 glass olive oil
flour

breadcrumbs

Remove the head and the guts from the pilchards, leaving the tail. Marinate the fish in a half-water and half-vinegar mix for 1 hour. Drain it and let it dry. Flour the fish and deep-fry it in olive oil. Place the fish apart. Add the vinegar to the pan with the olive oil and heat it to make a sauce. Sprinkle the fish with the hot sauce and some breadcrumps. Serve cold with white wine.

Cod with potatoes and peppers

Ingredients for 4 servings:
1k cod
300g potatoes
2 green peppers
½ glass olive oil
salt
pepper

Cut the cod into medium pieces and rinse them until soft. Remove the skin and the bones. Into a pan, place alternate layers of cod, potato slices and pepper stripes. Add salt, pepper and half a glass of olive oil. Cover the pan and let it simmer for 40 minutes.

Eggplant parmigiana

Ingredients for 4 servings:
4 big eggplants
1 onion
4 peeled tomatoes
4 boiled eggs
200g grated pecorino cheese
breadcrumbs
olive oil
salt

pepper

Slice the eggplants, deep-fry them in hot olive oil and leave apart. Slice the onion and slightly sauté into some of the olive oil where you fried the eggplants. Add the tomatoes without the seeds, salt and pepper and let the sauce cook for 10 minutes at medium heat. Into a baking pan, place alternate layers of eggplants, sauce, slices boiled eggs and grated pecorino cheese. Finish with a layer of sauce and sprinkle some cheese and breadcrumbs on top. Bake until golden. Let it cool for 15 minutes before serving.

Eggplants in sour-sweet sauce

Ingredients for 4 servings:
4 eggplants
1 onion
1 tablespoon walnuts chopped
1 tablespoon raisins
1 tablespoon pine nuts
1 tablespoon cocoa powder
1 ½ tablespoon sugar
½ glass white vinegar
cinnamon powder
olive oil
salt

pepper

Cut the eggplants into cubes and deep-fry them in hot olive oil. Cut the onion into fine slices and sauté them in a pan with half a glass of olive oil. Add the eggplants, the chopped walnuts, the raisins and the pine nuts, a pinch of cinnamon powder, the cocoa, salt and pepper. Add the sugar and the vinegar. Let it simmer in low heat for a couple of minutes. Serve cold.

Wheat with tomato meat sauce

Ingredients for 5 servings:
700g durum wheat
150g minced beef
150g minced pork
150g minced lamb
1 big onion
garlic
1k peeled tomatoes
1 glass red wine
1 chili pepper
1 cinnamon stick
salt

pepper

Leave the durum wheat in water for 48 hours. Cut the onion into fine slices, chop the chili pepper and sauté them together. Add the meat, sauté for a while and finish it with the wine. Add the chopped tomatoes, salt, pepper and cook at low heat for 1 hour. Boil the wheat in plenty of salty water. Drain and mix it with the meat sauce.

Mutton stew

Ingredients for 5 servings:
1k mutton meat
800g potatoes
300g onion
6 tomatoes
150g pecorino cheese in cubes
5 slices salami
1 chili pepper

To cook this stew, put all the ingredients into a clay pot, cover and place on the stove. Alternatively use a metal pan that can be sealed tight. Cut the mutton meat into pieces, peel the potatoes and place them into the pot. Add the onions, the tomatoes and the chili pepper all chopped, the pecorino cheese, the salami cut into small pieces, salt and fill ¼ of the pan with water. Cover it and let it cook for 2 hours. Serve with red wine.

Fish soup

Ingredients for 5 servings:
1k fresh fish (scorpion fish, groupers, sea bream, cuttlefish)
2 carrots
100g celery
½ onion chopped
2 garlic cloves
white wine
½ glass olive oil
1 chili pepper

salt

Remove the heads and tails and boil them in water with the celery and the carrots. Clean and rinse the fish and cut it into medium pieces. In a pan with olive oil, sauté the onion and the garlic. Add the fish, sprinkling it with a few drops of white vinegar. Add the chili pepper and salt. Mix the soup with the fish broth. Let it cook at medium heat for 10 minutes. Serve with garlic flavor croutons.

Snail soup

Ingredients for 4 servings:
1k snails
500g tomato sauce
5 garlic cloves
olive oil

Put the snails into a wicker basket with some wine leaves and let them purge for 2 days. When ready, wash the snails carefully and place them into a pan. Cover them with water and place them on strong heat, to avoid the snails' coming of their shell. Boil for a few minutes, remove from heat and rinse them with fresh water. Heat the tomato sauce with the olive oil and the garlic in a pan, add the snails and let them cook for a few minutes.

Pitta with tomatoes and olives

Ingredients for 6 servings:
600g flour
30g beer yeast
1k peeled tomatoes
2 garlic cloves
5 anchovy fillets
100g pitted olives
1 tablespoon capers
½ tablespoon parsley chopped
150g tuna in olive oil
½ glass olive oil

"Pitta" is a kind of cake made with bread dough and filled with various ingredients.

Prepare a soft dough with the flour, the yeast, a pinch of salt and some water. Let it stay in a warm place for 1 hour.

Meanwhile, chop the tomatoes, the garlic and the parsley. Put them into a pan with some olive oil and cook them for 5 minutes. Remove from heat and let it cool. In another pan with half a glass of olive oil, heat the anchovy fillets until they melt, add the chopped olives, the capers and the tuna.

Cut the dough into 2 equal pieces. Place one into a round baking pan and press it with your fingers to make a layer that covers the bottom and the sides of the pan. Add the 2 sauces on top of the dough and mix them. Roll the other piece of dough into a round sheet and place it on top of the pan, to cover the pitta. Make some little holes with a fork on top and bake in the oven at 180°C until golden.

Pitta with ricotta cheese

Ingredients for 6 servings:
300g fresh ricotta cheese
50g salty ricotta grated cheese
100g salami
3 boiled eggs
olive oil

Prepare the dough as described in the previous recipe.

For the filling, mix the fresh ricotta and the salty ricotta cheese with a bit of olive oil.

Cut the dough into 2 equal pieces. Place one into a round baking pan and press it with your fingers to make a layer that covers the bottom and the sides of the pan. Spread half of the cheese mix on the dough sheet. Make a layer of salami slices and a layer of boiled egg slices. Spread the rest of the cheese mix on top. Roll the other piece of dough into a round sheet and place it on top of the pan, to cover the pitta. Make some little holes with a fork on top and bake in the oven at 180° until golden. Serve cold.

Fava beans and chicory soup

Ingredients for 4 servings:
500g fava beans (peeled)
200g chicory
olive oil
pecorino cheese
pepper

Place the fava beans into slightly salty water over night. Put the beans into a pan, cover them with water and let them boil at low heat. Cut the chicory into medium pieces, boil them for 1 minute and add them to the beans, before they are completely cooked. To finish add olive oil, pepper and pecorino cheese to taste.

Rabbit with potatoes

Ingredients for 8 servings:
1 rabbit
4 garlic cloves
200g green olives
50g capers in vinegar
1 heart of celery
3 peppers
2 mature tomatoes
4 medium potatoes
½ glass white vinegar
extra-virgin olive oil
salt
pepper

Cut the meat into medium pieces, rinse it and place it into a pan with hot olive oil. Cook until golden. In another pan sauté in olive oil the garlic, the tomatoes and the celery all chopped, the olives and the capers. Mix all, add salt and pepper to taste and let it simmer for a while. Add the peppers cut into stripes and the potatoes cut into cubes. Let it cook for a few more minutes and add the meat. Pour the vinegar and half glass of hot water. Cook for another 30 minutes. Serve in room temperature.

Braised kid goat

Ingredients for 8 servings:
3k kid goat
150g lard
4 big lemons
1k potatoes
5 carots
rosemary
sage
salt
pepper

Braised kid goat is a typical traditional recipe which is normally cooked for Easter.
Cut the meat into medium pieces and keep apart the entrails. Rinse well and place it into a big hot pan at strong heat. When it starts drying, add the lard, salt and pepper, rosemary and sage and let it cook at medium heat for 30 minutes. Move it every now and then to avoid sticking at the bottom of the pan and add some water if necessary. Add the entrails, the potatoes and the carrots all cut into pieces and cook for another 30 minutes. At the end raise the heat until golden and finish with lemon juice. Serve hot.

Fried prickly pears' peel

Ingredients for 6 servings:
500g prickly pears' peel
2 eggs
flour
breadcrumbs
olive oil
salt

Choose prickly pears with nice, thick skin, peel them and rinse them under tap water carefully. Use a knife to cut out the thorns and cut the peel into medium pieces. Scramble the eggs into a bowl with a pinch of salt. Flour the peel, then pass it from the egg and finally from the bread crumbs. Deep-fry into olive oil until golden. Drain well using kitchen paper and serve hot.

The Mafia Codes

Here is a list of some of the most important codes that have been found by the Police in Italy as well as in other parts of the world. These codes have revealed the, almost religious, rules of one of the most powerful Mafia organizations:

In 1926 and in 1927 two codes were found in Plati and Gioiosa Jonica respectively (undecoded).

In 1963 the codes of San Giorgio, Sant' Eufemia and Gioia Tauro were found in the accommodation of Angelo Violanti (undecoded).

In 1971 the code of Toronto and four years later the code of Presinaci were found (undecoded).

On the 27th October 1980, a code about the ritual of affiliation of Domenica Nirta was recovered in Giralang, Australia.

In June 1987 the first code about the rituals of the "Santa" was found in the house of Giuseppe Chila, a member of the 'Ndrangheta, in Pellaro.

In December 1987, the code of Raffaele Alvaro for the rituals of the Camorra was found in Nailsworth Building.

In 1989, the code of Reggio Calabria was recovered from capo Giuseppe Chilla. In this code the society of the Mafia as well as the characteristics of the organization and its rules are described.

In 1990, the codes of Rosarno, Lamezia, Terme and Vellefiorita were found (undecoded).

In 2013, after the arrest of Gianni Cretarola, accused for the murder of Vincenzo Femia, in Rome, the investigators found in his house three pages in writing of a code composed using the Greek and Latin alphabet along with special symbols. When decoded it was found to be a code of 'Ndrangheta, where amongst others the ritual of baptism was described.

These codes were and are still memorized by heart by the members of the society.

Suggestion:

For anyone who would be interested in learning more and in depth about the 'Ndrangheta, there is no better author than the anti-mafia judge Nicola Gratteri.

CPSIA information can be obtained
at www.ICGtesting.com
Printed in the USA
LVOW01s1147151215
466715LV00028B/2267/P

9 781502 374912